T0045518

Santo and I

Gavin Stolten

Illustrated by Marjorie Scott

My name is Paco.
Santo is my grandson.
We live in Greenvale.
I've lived here since I was little.

Sometimes Santo and I walk down Main Street together.

I remember what Main Street was like when I was little.

Sometimes I take Santo to the park.

I remember what the park was like
when I was little.

Sometimes Santo and I go to the lake together.

I remember what the lake was like
when I was little.

Sometimes I take Santo to school.

I remember what the school was like
when I was little.

Sometimes Santo and I go to a baseball game together.

I remember what baseball games were like when I was little.

Sometimes Santo and I help in the hardware store.

I remember what the store was like when Santo's dad was little.